A SECOND APPEAL

A Consideration of Freedom and Social Justice

Daphne M. Rolle

University Press of America,® Inc.
Lanham · Boulder · New York · Toronto · Plymouth, UK

Copyright © 2010 by
University Press of America,® Inc.
4501 Forbes Boulevard
Suite 200
Lanham, Maryland 20706
UPA Acquisitions Department (301) 459-3366

Estover Road
Plymouth PL6 7PY
United Kingdom

Library of Congress Control Number: 2009938306
ISBN: 978-0-7618-4961-2 (paperback : alk. paper)
eISBN: 978-0-7618-4962-9

CONTENTS

Preface

The time has come that philosophers consider what the *future* of philosophy will be. It is getting more and more difficult to argue convincingly to non-philosophers that our discipline is not obsolete and that it does hold great value for those who never intend to pursue academic degrees in philosophy. The benefit of critically examining our lives is undeniable. The discipline of philosophy has much to teach us about what questions are important to ask, as well as how to identify important implications that follow from the beliefs and practices we establish. Everyone is affected, both individually and as members of the collective group, by the decisions we make. Therefore, this work is addressed to everyone. It is an appeal for all to consider the relevance of learning to identify and ponder those fundamental questions whose answers shape worldviews and civilization. Using the methodology the discipline of philosophy offers, we can inform and guide public discourse in the way Socrates urged long ago—adopting philosophy as a tool of praxis.

As I thought about the shape this appeal would take, I decided perhaps the best approach would be to invite others to engage in discourse about two very pressing concerns of our day—freedom and social justice. We are presently engaged in numerous conflicts regarding each and yet we seem to be lacking a necessary degree of clarity when it comes to defining and understanding either one. Whether it is a conversation about the merits of democracy or a debate about what constitutes socialist policy, as we "fight" for freedom and pursue social justice, it is not clear we fully understand what constitutes freedom and social justice. As we are trying to decide how best to deal with the mistakes of the past and how to develop an infrastructure for the future, we would be best served by considering the larger, long-term goal. We cannot expect to make significant progress without a vision. In general, this is true, even more so within the context of a democracy. The people must be a part of establishing and articulating the collective vision—a clear view of freedom and social justice. Currently it should be quite apparent that we cannot leave this important task to the politicians or media. It is my hope that after even a brief consideration we will recognize that the individual responsibilities we all bear to participate in our democracy prevents us from shifting the work that must be done into the hands of others—preachers, politicians, activists, or anyone other than ourselves. What follows are my reflections on freedom and social justice. I offer them as an invitation to engage in a discourse that seeks clarity regarding our understanding of and paths to achieving each of these goals.

Framed as an invitation, the brevity of the work is intended and is modeled after David Walker's *Appeal to the Coloured Citizens of the World*. I begin with an analysis of Walker's work to highlight the fact that we as a nation have struggled with articulating a clear and defensible concept of freedom from the very beginning. Moreover, it is one of the tasks for philosophers, especially those who do African-American philosophy, to review historical documents and re-present them highlighting their philosophical value. By doing so we are offering them as valuable intellectual resources for present times. Performing a philosophical investigation of Walker's *Appeal* also illustrates how his "incendiary" text contributed to the public discourse of the time and significantly impacted the intellectual as well as social and political terrain.

One of the most important features of Walker's *Appeal* is its timelessness. Because Walker is addressing a number of the most fundamental questions we as humans must face, his work has a universal appeal. What does it really mean to be free? What does democracy have to offer us? What does it mean to treat another as your equal? Who is God and what is his character? These are questions that can be and are asked by everyone. Moreover, they are questions that shape our worldviews and influence our decisions and practices.

Also addressed in this second appeal are the problems that arise when we allow subjective theological interpretations, what I will call identity theologies, to take the lead in shaping our concept of social justice. We see evidence of these problems in the examples of the 'Christian right' and some liberation theologies. It is very important that a serious treatment of such phenomena be part of our current public discourse. We, as citizens of this nation, must participate in the shaping of our concepts of freedom and social justice if we ever hope to experience their fruition. We must dedicate ourselves to service and participate in the practice and further development of our democratic ideals. We must get engaged.

> Daphne M. Rolle
> Indianapolis, IN
> May, 2009

Article I
An Analysis of David Walker's *Appeal*

"They promise them freedom, while they themselves are slaves of depravity — for a man is a slave to whatever has mastered him." 2 Peter 2:19[1]

David Walker, an early nineteenth century black abolitionist shocked America with his indictment of American slavery and slaveholders. His proclamations regarding the wretched state of colored persons in America and his subsequent call for them to rise up in unity and kill all who would perpetuate the institution of slavery alarmed everyone, prompting several southern state legislatures to establish laws prohibiting the literacy of colored persons. Walker anticipated that his pamphlet would not be well-received by those who had an interest in seeing slavery continue. He also suspected criticism would be offered by a number of his own brethren who he believed were ignorant enough to accept that their conditions could not be bettered. However, the negative response of others involved in abolitionist activities, was perhaps not anticipated but was immediate and did much to counteract the impact of Walker's *Appeal*. Several of the same people who supported the spirit of revolution leading to the independence of this country from British oppression could not embrace the notion of a revolution for colored persons fighting against the unjustifiable oppression of slavery. The concept of *revolution* did not apply as an appropriate response in the case of slavery. Even among those sympathetic to abolition, there was absent the acceptance of human accountability for slavery. Slavery was then, much what it is today, a miserable and unfortunate institution that victimized America. As such, even rebellion against slavery was unacceptable because both revolution and rebellion would likely require the sacrifice of lives, and the freedom from oppression for colored persons did not warrant such a sacrifice. Consequently, other abolitionists distanced themselves from Walker, joining those who condemned his pamphlet as "incendiary," "divisive," and "harmful."

David Walker had a very different view of slavery and its consequence – creating the world's most wretched race of people. His *Appeal to the Colored Citizens of the World* gives us a most articulate, if not persuasive, argument for insurrection as a response to the oppression of slavery. Walker's insurrection gains its sanction from being grounded in Christian theology. Walker argues that the freedom God intended for man is just as befitting for the colored persons of the world as it was for the founders of the United States of America. Freedom is that unalienable right granted by God for all mankind to enjoy. Given his Christian theological grounding for the securing of freedom, what is interesting about his concept of freedom is that it is not based upon the salvation of the individual as one might expect. It is rather defined solely in social and political terms. As Walker discusses the *wretchedness* of the colored persons in the world, particularly in America, a picture of what constitutes true human bondage and freedom emerges. It is a picture that is quite provocative, and its study can provide us with valuable guidance as we wrestle today with developing our notions of freedom and its value.

Walker speaks about the importance of and right to freedom of both mind and body, suggesting that such is the *natural state* of human beings, and agreeing with the principles articulated in the United States Constitution and Declaration of Independence. The specific crime against morality of slavery is that the Negro was judged to be less than human. Walker called it the "insupportable insult" of American slavery. He begins by repeatedly drawing to his readers' attention the fact of the humanity of the Negro. Walker says, "[those] who can dispense with prejudice long enough to admit that we are *men*, notwithstanding our improminent noses and woolly heads, and believe that we feel for our fathers, mothers, wives and children, as well as the whites do for theirs"[2] will see that slavery must be abolished. Walker is writing in the 1830's at a time when the country had just gone through a very significant period in which the principles and boundaries of human freedom had been established. He believed that if the humanity of the Negro could be established, then the necessary conditions of freedom would obviously apply. Walker establishes the humanity of the Negro by pointing out their similarities to others acknowledged as fully human and by appealing to the creation of man as given in Holy Scripture. Many others involved in the cause of abolition had done likewise; so this was not unique to Walker. Walker, however, was quite distinctive in his method of presentation and the particular structure of his argument.

There are three distinctive features of Walker's *Appeal* that prompted it to be labeled incendiary subsequently leading to its ban which resulted in its dismissal from collections of noted historical documents for well over a century. The first distinctive feature is his characterization of God. For Walker, God is one who is interested and actively involved in the day-to-day lives of his people. The second is his critique of the character of the white enlightened Christian Americans. He raises the question of their moral character suggesting that they are not the moral equals of the slaves they despise. He concludes that they are not and pronounces them *natural enemies* of the Negro, thereby introducing a key concept in his work. The third is his call for slaves to take up arms and kill their masters and all who would continue to see them held in bondage. The premise he assumes is that death is preferable to the wretchedness experienced as a slave. As far as he can see, insurrection is the only way slavery will end.

Walker's characterization of God is critical in that God provides the standard by which to measure human progress. God is Creator of all that is and he is not a God of distinction. Walker believes God to have among other characteristics omniscience, omnipotence, omnipresence, perfect goodness, mercy, love and justice. It is God's justice that is one of the most important qualities for Walker. The nature of God's justice is such that it *requires* him to be involved and active in man's day-to-day affairs, and one of God's concerns is how we interact with one another. It is not the case that God merely keeps track of the individual's actions so that the proper reward or punishment may be handed out at the end of the person's life. God makes his judgments on a day-to-day basis and may very well find it necessary to reward or punish the individual in his/her present life.

Walker's God is one who aids the righteous and punishes the wicked. Humans have been created in God's image and must recognize his authority over their lives. Humans have also been given free wills and can therefore make choices about who will have authority over them. The choice they make regarding this matter of authority is the standard by which God judges an individual to be righteous or wicked. God allows man to make his own decisions, but the righteous will recognize the need to submit to God's will and commands. For them the reward is God's blessings; however God's justice requires him to repay wickedness with wrath.

The person who falsely believes he has authority over his own life and chooses to disregard the commands of God is the wicked man according to Walker. It is fairly early on in his pamphlet that Walker makes it clear that in his eyes, and in the eyes of God, one cannot help but see that the whites who allow the continuance of the institution of American slavery are wicked—the slaveholders and slave traders being the worst. In the preamble, however, Walker takes it a step further and refers to the white slave holders as "our enemies by nature." What made their wickedness so terrible that they became the *natural enemies* of the wretched? It is their conscious hypocrisy. In fact, they were "enlightened Christians" who used intellectual arguments to support slavery.

The Enlightenment Walker refers to is that period during the eighteenth century experienced by the leading intellectuals of the United States of America that inspired the American Revolution, the Bill of Rights and the Declaration of Independence. It is that period when reason was pronounced to have the power to accurately define the individual, the society, the state, and morality. Our understanding of what an individual is and what he/she needs changed at that time. Our understanding of political ideals and worthwhile political ventures changed. Our understanding of human activity as a whole, from religion to economic pursuits, underwent a radical shift during this time of enlightenment, and we pledged ourselves to democracy, classical liberalism, and capitalism. It is these enlightened people who have come to understand the power of reason, its influence and its improving force that Walker charges with disregarding reason and glorying in their wickedness when it came to the question of slavery.

The institution of slavery presented the early leaders of this nation with a dilemma. Economic interests were at odds with the new democratic ideals, particularly the one found in our Declaration of Independence proclaiming *"all men*

*are created equal, that they are endowed by their Creator with certain unalien-
able Rights."* There was a choice to be made. Ultimately the financial stability
of the new nation took precedence over the "self-evident" notions of universal
human rights. That they were identified as self-evident merely highlights the fact
that when it came to the question of slavery, the disregarding of reason was deliberate. To make matters worse, the slave was not only denied liberty, the pursuit of happiness, and life in some instances, the slave was also denied education. The slave was allowed to have no knowledge of either the God or Laws of
Nature that framed the concept of self-determination evident in both the Declaration of Independence and later the United States Constitution. This deliberate
denial of access to education regarding the most fundamental aspects of human
life convinced Walker of the evil residing in the *"enlightened Christians"* who
supported slavery. He speaks of them as "those whose greatest earthly desires
are to keep us in abject ignorance and wretchedness,"[3] marking the colored people of the United States of America as the most wretched creatures who have
ever lived on the face of the earth.

The firm conviction held by Walker that the whites who supported slavery
were the natural enemies of the colored people is what prevented him from ac-
cepting moral suasion as a proper method for seeking abolition. Many of the
suasionist arguments were directed against slavery as an evil institution that was
in a strange sense independent of actual individuals supporting it. Slavery was a
faceless institution that claimed everyone, slave and slaveholder alike, as its
victims. Walker, on the contrary, does not just indict slavery and the racism that
justified it. He puts a face on the ideology supporting the institution of slavery,
and that face is white.

The moral suasionists such as William Whipper and William Lloyd Garri-
son were erring in trying to appeal to moral sensibilities in whites that had become insensate. The proponents of slavery were simply too evil, their characters
too corrupted to be persuaded by rational and/or moral arguments against slavery. Furthermore, their "enlightenment" showed that they were intentional in
their immorality. They had become children of the devil and enemies of all
good. Walker says, "If it were possible, would they not dethrone Jehovah and
seat themselves upon his throne? I therefore . . . advance my suspicion of them,
whether they are *as good by nature* as we are or not."[4] For Walker, the only rea-
sonable response to such evil and deformed character was insurrection. These
natural enemies of the slave, of God, and of freedom were not to be persuaded.
They must therefore be forcibly subdued or killed.

There was never a question for Walker about the value of freedom. Freedom is that natural state intended by God for man; as such, seeking it is certainly
worth giving one's life if necessary. The slave in the United States was so far
from being free, was so wretched, that death would be an improvement upon
their condition. For Walker it was a simple case of kill or be killed, but you cannot remain a slave.

The wretchedness of colored persons in general, free and enslaved, within
the context of American democracy was equally well established according to

Walker. In his *Appeal* he identifies slavery as the institutional source of the miseries of Negroes, but he holds responsible all, both black and white, who encourage, participate in, and allow for its continuance. Anyone who fails to fight for the freedom of the slave is at least allowing slavery to continue. Although slavery was actuated by the avarice of the white slave owners, the colored persons must share responsibility for the perpetuation of slavery due to their compliance and unwillingness to participate in rebellion and insurrection. Walker was insistent that the humanity of the Negro, free or slave, should provide them with the unquenchable desire for true freedom, and that a longing for that freedom should spur them to seek it at whatever cost. According to Walker, "Man is a peculiar creature—he is the image of his God, though he may be subjected to the most wretched condition upon earth, yet the spirit and feeling which constitute the creature, man, can never be entirely erased from his breast."[5] Walker held up as an example the successful slave rebellion in Haiti in 1804 as the most natural response to slavery. Walker articulates, however, a truly enlightened response—rebellion as a duty to God.

Walker's argument in favor of insurrection is based on the following assumptions: the Bible is historical fact, God is the Creator of all that is, God is not a god of distinction, God is perfectly just, and American slavery is evil. A fundamental argument of Walker's *Appeal* is found in his preamble. The argument is:

> 1) If God allows slavery, is he a god of justice?
> 2) No, yet God is perfectly just.
> 3) Therefore, he will not allow slavery to continue.

It is on the basis of this argument that Walker calls colored citizens of the world to arms. A few years earlier in London, Robert Wedderburn, made a similar insurrectionist appeal.[6] Man must fight with God for the heavenly cause of freedom. If choosing sordid avarice over the natural and moral laws of God is what makes a white man evil, what makes a colored wretch evil is that he/she refuses, for whatever reason, to fight for the right to call no one but Jesus Christ master. The emphasis here is that *true freedom* is a heavenly cause; it is what God desires for mankind.

Walker pronounces, "The man who would not fight under our Lord and Master Jesus Christ, in the glorious and heavenly cause of freedom and of God ought to be kept with all of his children or family, in slavery, or in chains, to be butchered by his cruel enemies."[7] He believes this to be categorically true; however, the value of freedom in a Republican Democracy was especially highlighted. It is this full freedom described by the founders of America that Walker wanted for the Negro. He was not just seeking release from bondage (the freedom intended by God), but full rights of citizenship (the American concept of freedom).

For Walker, true freedom could only be experienced when both physical and psychological restraints were removed and colored citizens could participate in the religious, political and economic activities freely experienced by others recognized as citizens of the United States. He agreed with the sentiment expressed in the Declaration of Independence that those who recognize "the separate and equal station to which the Laws of Nature and of Nature's God entitle them" ought to be willing to pledge their lives while seeking its procurement. Walker took no issue with the ideals of democracy as articulated in the nation's founding documents. He merely believed the Negro should demand an equal level of participation.

Walker was especially critical of those political leaders who were staunch defenders of the ideals of American democracy, but at the same time supported the continuation of the institution of slavery. Two such figures of which he made special note were Thomas Jefferson and Henry Clay. Jefferson as one of the founding fathers and the author of America's most revered documents had too large an audience, and his words carried too much weight for his pronouncement regarding slavery and the Negro race to be taken lightly. When Jefferson spoke in support of slavery and when he advanced his suspicions regarding the inferiority of the Negro race, it made no small impact on how society thought about these issues.[8] Walker says of Jefferson,

> "A much greater philosopher the world never afforded, [he] has in truth injured us more, and has been as great a barrier to our emancipation as anything that has ever been advanced against us . . . Mr. Jefferson's remarks respecting us, have sunk deep into the hearts of millions of the whites, and never will be removed this side of eternity."[9]

Jefferson epitomized the conscious hypocrisy of the enlightened American idealist.

Jefferson was also one of the first to raise the issue of the colonization of free blacks. He expressed the view that because of the egregious harms experienced by blacks under slavery, a peaceful integration of the two races (white and black) would never be possible. There were a number of others who shared this view. However, Walker was very skeptical of their true motives. He believed it was the colonization plan that illustrated the fact it was a commitment to profit, not principle, to which the hypocritical Americans had pledged themselves. In 1816, the American Colonization Society (ACS) was established by a number of men who believed colonization was the only viable option for the placement of free blacks if the Union was to be preserved. Among those founding members was Henry Clay, Speaker of the House of Representatives and later Secretary of State under President John Adams. Clay was a very prominent politician and effective statesman. He is credited with shaping the history of the United States Congress and was named one of the five greatest Senators in American history in 1957. In fact, Clay was the first person to lie in state in the U.S. Capitol upon his death in 1852.

Clay advocated the colonization of free blacks to Liberia for several reasons, none of which had to do with the eventual abolishment of slavery but everything to do with its continuance. Here we see the true motive behind the colonization plan according to Walker. One of the most pressing reasons to support the colonization plan was that the settlement of free blacks in Liberia would help prevent the intermingling of slaves with free blacks here in the United States, thereby averting attempts of revolt. Between 1800 and 1815, there had been four slave revolts attempted. All of them were suppressed, but one occurring in 1811 in Louisiana involved approximately 500 slaves. It is the largest slave revolt in U.S. history. Many whites, both northern and southern, did not want to see such activity continue, and colonization was seen as a preventative measure.

Another reason for supporting the colonization plan was to prevent the negative economic effects of having free blacks enter the work force in the North. Between 1790 and 1810, there was a significant increase in the population of free blacks. This increase was of particular concern to those looking after the interests of working class whites, as well as those who feared racial mixing. It was never the intention of these statesmen to allow the Negro to participate fully in the social and political activities of the country.

However, the reason for which Walker takes Clay to task is his belief that the removal of free blacks from American society was the "right" thing to do. Clay expressed sentiments similar to Jefferson's regarding the impossibility of assimilation into American culture because of the "unconquerable prejudice" against Negroes. He also thought it was best not to expose slaves to even the idea of freedom in the American society. A motive of ACS expressed by Elias B. Caldwell, Clerk of the Supreme Court and secretary of ACS, indicates that the colonization plan was in part an effort to "keep [slaves] in the lowest state of degradation and ignorance. The nearer you bring them to the condition of brutes, the better chance do you give them of possessing their apathy."[10] By removing free blacks as examples of freedom, the likelihood of the slaves developing a yearning for freedom which they could never attain decreases. This was seen as an act of benevolence and as such received financial support from the federal government as well as a few blacks.

Walker rejects all of these reasons and points out that in the end the ACS had as its primary agenda securing the American institution of slavery. He quotes another founding member John Randolph who said of the colonization plan, "so far from being connected with abolition of slavery, the measure proposed would prove one of the greatest securities to enable the master to keep in possession his own property."[11] That most of the founding members of the society were slave holders only demonstrated the fact that this was not a plan prompted by benevolence but by avarice.

Walker sees America as belonging to the Negroes as much as it does to whites. He argues against colonization based upon the principle of fairness. The slaves, as first tillers of the land, have an interest in America that is at least equal to that of whites. Furthermore, there were Negro soldiers who helped fight in the Revolutionary War, and their sacrifices and efforts should be noted. He rejects that there are practical or economic reasons for promoting colonization and points to the numbers of immigrants entering America and being sustained as his

support. The Negro belongs to America and America belongs in part to the Negro; the price paid for such a relationship is the tears and blood
of thousands. They have a right to remain in America, and it is in their best interest to do so, since notwithstanding the *practices* of enlightened Americans. It
is the place where the gospel is free and wisdom is the guide in principle.

The very reason the first settlers came to America, the freedom to practice
their religion, is the reason Walker wants Negroes to stay. Walker's commitment to Christian and democratic principles was unshakable. He was determined
to see the democratic enterprise in America succeed. Slavery must therefore be
abolished since slavery is incompatible with both Christianity and democracy.
Religion and its practice are to serve as the cornerstone of a man's life. God has
given man a dispensation of his Divine will—man is meant to spread the message of the gospel. Walker says of the white Christian Americans, preachers
included, that the way they practice the religion of Jesus Christ leads one to believe "it was a plan fabricated by themselves and the devils to oppress [the Ne-
gro]."[12] In short, they had defiled it by putting personal profit before preaching
the gospel.

In the last two articles of his *Appeal,* Walker addresses the ways in which
the practice of American slavery violates Christian and democratic principles.
His remarks regarding these issues will be treated in subsequent chapters of this
text. As was stated earlier, Walker's concept of freedom is not based upon salvation but is one essentially tied to one's social and political status. For Walker,
slavery requires physical bondage. Anything else is merely wretchedness. Consequently, freedom from physical restraint prohibits the use of the term slavery
to accurately describe one's existential condition. Such an account of slavery
and freedom make the efforts to secure freedom for oneself or others political in
nature. Slavery or any form of bondage or discrimination for that matter and the
securing of freedom are not political problems. They are problems of values. We
are slaves to the values that have mastered us. We must begin with this realiza-
tion as we form an appropriate concept of freedom.

Notes

1. This and all subsequent references to scripture has been taken from the New Interna-
tional Version.
2. David Walker, Appeal to the Coloured Citizens of the World (New York: Hill and
Wang, 1965), p. 4.
3. Ibid., p.2.
4. Ibid., p.17.
5. Ibid., p.61.
6. See Ian McCalman (ed.) The Horrors of Slavery and Other Writings by Robert Wedderburn (Princeton: Markus Wiener Publishers, 1991), p. 45.
7. Walker, Appeal, p.12.

8. See Thomas Jefferson's Notes on the State of Virginia (Richmond, VA: J.W. Randolph, 1853).

9. Walker, Appeal, p. 27-28.

10. Ibid., p. 52.

11. Ibid., p. 55. A register of the ACS records can be found in the Manuscript Division of the Library of Congress. It is a very interesting read.

12. Ibid., p. 35.

Article II
Against Identity Theology

"Each man's life is but a breath. Man is a mere phantom as he goes to and fro:
He bustles about in vain . . ." Psalm 39: 5-6

Much of the theology we find both past and present has been shaped by particular social conditions and political identities. In their varied forms they represent what I will refer to as identity theologies. While they each pick out different aspects of identity as a lens through which theology is interpreted, what they all share is the implication that the theology of Christianity is best understood only after it has been contextualized. Identity theologies assert God's preference and special concern for the interests of a particular group often identified by race, ethnicity, or socio-economic status. Some current examples of such theologies are black theology, liberation theology, and "social justice" theology.

We see this promotion of an identity theology at work in David Walker's *Appeal.* According to Walker, the freedom God intends for humans to enjoy can most clearly be understood within the context of democratic ideals. However, the intended universality of that freedom can best be understood from the perspective of the Negro—the oppressed and enslaved. Those who are able to identify and sympathize with this group will be the recipients of God's grace. Walker uses the Old Testament as the basis for his brand of liberation theology which emphasizes the right of revolution. As has been previously mentioned, Walker's concept of freedom, while theologically grounded, is not based upon the individual's salvation but rather is defined in social and political terms. This perhaps makes Walker the first African-American to articulate a black liberation theology.

Article III of Walker's *Appeal* states that "pure and undefiled religion, such as was preached by Jesus Christ and his apostles, is hard to be found in all the earth."[1] He believed that any departure from the faith and the charge given by God would corrupt the practice of religion. Following Walker's own standard of a pure and undefiled religion, we can see that Jesus did not direct his efforts to those in bondage alone. It is the jailer in the account of the apostles Paul and Silas' release from prison who is saved and set free.[2]

However, the Christian Americans are seemingly beyond redemption according to Walker. Because they intentionally prevented Negroes from worshiping God rather than trying to convert them, while at the same time they sent missionaries out to the "heathens" of the world, Walker is convinced that their 'cups are nearly full.' Of the pretend preachers Walker remarks:

> They being preachers of the gospel of Jesus Christ, if it [slavery] were any harm, they would surely preach against their oppression and do their utmost to erase it from the country; not only in one or two cities, but one continual cry would be raised in all parts of this confederacy, and would cease only with the complete overthrow of the system of slavery, in every part of the country.[3]

The American preachers of Christianity, however, use their position to endorse slavery by arguing it is the appropriate condition for the Negro. Revolution is not an option for the Negroes for they must be obedient to their masters. This hypocrisy indicates a religion shaped by conditions, circumstances, and self-interest rather than enduring and unchanging principles. Given God's perfectly just character, Walker is convinced that the Americans' destruction is sure, and he gives numerous dire pronouncements to that effect. He does not seem to believe in even the possibility of their redemption—the possibility which is at the heart of the pure and simple message preached by Jesus and his apostles.

Time and again Walker argues that the gospel of Christ is not one that makes distinctions among men. All need to be saved. Those who preach a gospel of distinction are mocking God, and he asks "can there be a greater absurdity in nature, and particularly in a free republican country?"[4] One is left to wonder what the basis is for God's preferences or distinctions based upon social conditions. Walker argues that God has no preference for color—we are all created equally. Why then does God have a preference for the oppressed—especially those who are complicit in their own oppression as Walker clearly points out? Salvation, which is the objective of the gospel message, is made available to all for all have sinned and fallen short of God's glory. It is impossible to be worthy of salvation based upon human action. The standard for righteousness is Christ himself, not other men.

Walker's failure was to not base the concept of freedom on salvation. He rather based it on particular social and political conditions and the 'distinction' of being oppressed. This is the same mistake made by present day activists. The message of the gospel gets lost in the march for justice. By making economic justice and political empowerment the theological emphasis, the fact that Jesus really does intend for freedom, justice and peace to be enjoyed by everyone, including those who have been oppressors, gets lost. The fundamental conflict found in "pure and undefiled" Christian theology is not between the oppressor and the oppressed. It is between light and darkness. The message of the gospel is not best understood through the lens of a particular socio-historic context; it is best understood from the eternal perspective of Christ. The emphasis of Christ's own message was on the individual's salvation due to the accompanying eternal implications. Christ was much more concerned about where the individual would spend eternity than he was about that individual's living conditions on earth. This is not to say that he was unconcerned with how one lives here on earth, but that concern was clearly subordinate to one's eternal dwelling place.

Taking a closer look at current articulations of social justice theology, we see an effort to establish advocacy for social justice as the primary emphasis of the black church. It is known as the social gospel. Similar to the liberation theology that emerged as a formal movement in the 1960's social justice theology interprets Christian theology as primarily a message of securing liberty for the poor and oppressed because of God's special concern for this group. The New Testament is understood to be a message of social justice evidenced by the passage found in Luke that reads, "The Spirit of the Lord is on me, because he has anointed me to preach good news to the poor. He has sent me to proclaim freedom for the prisoners and recovery of sight for the blind, to release the oppressed."[5] The interpretation of prisoners and oppressed is understood quite literally. There are no subtle nuances to include those souls who are slaves to sin – those who are "free" and yet in bondage. Nor is there room for the slave held in bondage who yet experiences freedom.

The call is for people to engage in political activism in order to secure social justice. The specific appeal is often made to pastors of black churches of all denominations. They are called to be proactive in the procurement of social justice. The argument is that this is the proper role for the black church of today. The preferred method is to engage in social critique by confronting the injustice and bringing it to light for the public at large, and then to focus on changing the structures and policies that provide the basis for systemic oppression.

A theological enterprise such as this frames the most fundamental conflict as one between the oppressor and the oppressed. As a result, freedom, justice and peace are articulated primarily in political terms. One can perhaps even argue they are almost exclusively understood in political terms. Freedom, justice and peace are meant to be enjoyed by everyone. Consequently, economic justice through political empowerment is what all who are oppressed and disenfranchised should be seeking. It makes sense then that collaborations would be formed as differences are made subordinate to the larger goal. Universal freedom, justice and peace as the theological emphasis trumps all other doctrinal differences—denominational and at times perhaps even faith in the cases of Christian/Jewish or Christian/Muslim inter-faith collaborations.

A literal reading of the Bible indicates that the primary task to which God calls his people is not to secure justice for everyone. That would be an impossible task, so God is taking care of that himself. Justice will be brought to everyone at the time of Christ's return. God desires for his people to seek the salvation of others. Consequently, God calls those who are free to *do* justice. We are to do unto others as we would have them do unto us. This is what God requires of the church as the Body of Christ—not particular churches, not the black church. It is important for the Body of Christ to do justice because it is by communicating the availability of salvation to all that others will be drawn in and will receive the salvation that is necessary for the experience of true freedom. People must be drawn into the faith for it is through faith that eternal life is accessed, not through the experience of political freedom or acts of social justice. Individual salvation is the focus of biblical text.

In these current times where political and social conditions seem to change (quite drastically at times) on a frequent basis, the message of the church really should be simple and straight-forward. The message of the gospel is fundamentally a very simple message—"Repent and believe the good news."[6] The important choice is between Jesus or something/someone else, between light and darkness. The real point of the passage from Luke is not that liberty must be secured for the prisoners and the oppressed must be released. The point is that Jesus was sent to do this. The charge of the church is to lift Jesus up that others may be drawn to him so that *he* may set them free and release them from their bondage. Neither Walker nor the current day social gospel activists can free anyone in the most important sense of the word, *eternally*.

Identity theologies are simply inconsistent with Christ's own message. Jesus said, "You [men] judge by human standards; I pass judgment on no one."[7] Jesus died to forgive, not to judge. This essential part of his message gets clouded in identity theology, and if it is not communicated clearly, then the efforts made toward social justice are in vain. As Cornel West describes it, the social gospel becomes a powerful critique tied to abortive praxis.[8]

That fundamental democratic and Christian principles were set aside in favor of a commitment to self-interested individualism and economic gain by *enlightened Christians* is what Walker found impossible to reconcile. As he indicated, their practice of Christianity bore little resemblance to the gospel preached by Jesus. Rather they developed their own gospel, a social gospel, that more accurately represented their own values. In this case what we have is a theology shaped by cultural values rather than cultural values being shaped by theology understood as a fixed standard of truth. Similarly, the U.S. Constitution and actual practice of democracy bore little resemblance to the Declaration of Independence but instead reflected the actual political values of the times.

It is extremely useful and important to be able to identify the actual values at work—the ability to do so helps to explain the justifications of slavery put forward by the politicians, property owners, and preachers who favored slavery. It answers the perplexing question of how slavery was able to be sustained for so long in this nation founded upon the ideals of independence and individual freedom. It is not a very difficult task to show the obvious inconsistencies present amongst the leaders and founders of the nation and the accompanying heinous consequences. Walker was able to fairly accurately assess the situation. He also accurately identified the root of the problem—not slavery itself but the inconsistencies that gave rise to and maintained the institution. Ultimately the pragmatics of politics took precedence over the commitment to the purity of principles. It is however true that it is much easier to find the fault in others than to find it in ourselves.

Walker failed to recognize that the same fault he identified in the proponents of slavery existed to some degree in his own argument. While the specific values of Walker and those who would see slavery continue were markedly different, Walker with his political conception of freedom ultimately makes the same mistake of defining his policy in political terms, which are limited to human affairs, rather than practices more consistent with his principles authored by God. That is to say Walker misunderstands the essence of freedom which leads him to appeal to the slaves and proponents of freedom to participate in insurrection. Insurrection is in fact insupportable and incompatible with his own understanding of who God is.

If we take a close look at how Walker defines freedom, we can see how such an inconsistency develops. The notion of freedom as described by many abolitionists, not just Walker, consisted of the obvious freedom from constraints, both physical and psychological, freedom of employment opportunity, freedom from insult upon human dignity, and freedom to be educated. It is not so unlike our ideas of freedom today. There was also present the belief that a full notion of freedom spoke to a political state. The idea that all humans are born free and have inalienable rights that are somewhat political in nature was also present, i.e. ownership of assets, social justice, and authority or power in governance as is the case with democracy.

Both David Walker and British revolutionary Robert Wedderburn speak about the importance of and right to freedom of both mind and body, suggesting that such is the "natural state" of human beings.

> "Have I not the feelings of human nature within my breast? Oppression I can bear with patience, for it hath always been my lot; but when to this is added insult and reproach from the authors of miseries, I am forced to take up arms in my own defense."[9]

It should be noted that both of the staunch abolitionists who argued for insurrection mentioned above were in fact born free. They both, however, make repeated references to their shared experience with those held in bondage. The insult of being less than human applied to the race, not the physical/social condition of members of the race. Colored persons were "wretched beasts" as Walker puts it because of beliefs held about those of African descent, not because of their slave status.

Walker's project as defined by him was to prompt inquiry and investigation into the wretchedness of colored persons, free and enslaved, within the context of American democracy—the end of which is to argue the social and political equality of the Negro. Walker is sure of his theology and attributes slavery's continuance primarily to a lack of unity among colored persons, their ignorance, the false preachers of the gospel of Christ, and the hypocritical commitment to the principles of democracy of American statesmen. He is equally sure of the remedy for the moral ill of slavery—political unity, education, a true practice of Christianity, and consistency in application of democratic principles.

Walker, who seeks to ground everything in Christian theology, made a mistake—one that was prompted by his absolute commitment to securing social and political freedom for the Negro. What is missing from Walker's theology is that he fails to leave room for the enslaved person in physical bondage who does in fact experience true freedom. Walker's concept of freedom identifies freedom from physical constraints as a necessary condition for freedom and makes physical bondage a necessary condition for slavery. He also fails to recognize the similarity to the slave of the physically free, yet impoverished white person who is in many respects also a slave, and therefore also wretched. Freedom as understood in the biblical context is considered in a much broader context. God does not define freedom in political or social terms. God in fact allowed for numerous instances of slavery, oftentimes requiring the enslavement of his chosen people. If Walker would agree that God's nature and character are fixed, then God was a God of justice when the Hebrew people experienced 400 years of Egyptian slavery. Moreover, God's justice cannot be called into question centuries later because he allowed the particular American institution of slavery to last almost 100 years. Yet none of the stories describing the emancipation of the Hebrew peoples were stories of insurrection. In fact, time and again the New Testament advises slaves to be obedient to their masters.[10] Furthermore, it suggests that such obedience will allow for the experience of true freedom even when one is held in physical bondage. Far from such an interpretation, Walker seems to suggest that such teaching represents the malicious misguidance of those who are pretenders to Christianity.

It could be argued, however, that the direction for slaves to obey their masters is consistent with the spirit of Christ's teachings and is indeed compatible with the experience of true freedom. Walker himself points to the example of Joseph who started off in Egypt as a slave but ended up being second only to Pharaoh. If we follow this example, we see that Joseph was always *free* because he always acknowledged God as the ultimate authority. His destiny was determined by his obedience to God. The psalmist phrased it in this way, "I will walk about in freedom, for I have sought out your precepts."[11]

Paul, the great apostle and author of most of the New Testament, tells us that freedom is essentially to be free in Christ. This is to say that freedom is tied to an understanding of and belief in one's identity in Christ. Freedom begins with an internal understanding and does not require a particular physical condition. To place the emphasis of freedom on physical conditions and to call for the enslaved to take up arms in the name of justice are in the context of the Bible in opposition to living by the Spirit—hence they are rebellion against God.[12] As suggested by the psalmist, freedom is experienced because one understands the principles of God. As such the only power required for freedom is the power to live in obedience to God.

Walker is mistaken when he places additional criteria on the experience of freedom, and his derived method for securing freedom is misguided. Walker is guilty of putting forward a social gospel, shaped by personal values and particular interests, albeit a different gospel than that of the proponents of slavery. His valuation of social and political freedom moves him away from the literal reading of the scripture he supports in the beginning of his *Appeal*.

Walker was correct in much of his analysis, but his failure to maintain the consistency he required of others led him to plot an improper path to freedom for the Negro. The notion that freedom is not at its essence about political or social conditions but rather requires conformity to certain principles is not only to be found in the biblical context. Others such as Plato and Confucius both offer similar accounts of freedom. That freedom requires necessary boundaries in the form of principles or values is not novel. What sparks discussion and controversy are the particular restraints on freedom put forward.

Notes

1. Walker, Appeal, p. 35.
2. See Acts 16:25-34.
3. Walker, Appeal, p. 38.
4. Ibid., p. 43.
5. Luke 4:18.
6. Mark 1:15.
7. John 8:15.
8. See the discussion of Afro-American revolutionary Christianity in Cornel West's Prophecy Deliverance (Philadelphia: The Westminster Press,1982).
9. Ian McCalman, (ed.) The Horrors of Slavery and Other Writings by Robert Wedderburn (Princeton: Markus Wiener Publishers, 1991), p. 45.
10. See Walker's Appeal, p. 39. See also 1 Timothy 5 and Titus 3.
11. Psalm 119:45.
12. See Isaiah 59:12-13.

Article III
The Essence of Freedom

"If you hold to my teaching, you are really my disciples. Then you will know the truth, and the truth will set you free . . . So if the Son sets you free, you will be free indeed." John 8:31-32, 36

The essence of freedom within the context of Christianity is found in the concept of salvation. What Walker and the false preachers he so harshly criticized failed to realize was the fact that the individual's identity is fundamentally grounded in his/her relationship to Christ. God does not make distinctions among people when it comes to who he loves and who he wants to reconcile to himself. God saved guard and prisoner alike, virtuous woman and prostitute, working-class and government officials, Hebrew, Greek, Roman and Ethiopian. The Bible is full of diversity of social status, race, profession, and economic class in its examples of those God has saved by his grace. So Walker is absolutely right when it comes to the fact that God is no distinguisher of persons. It therefore seems odd that he would see white Christian supporters of slavery as beyond hope.

Walker, as has been earlier noted, understands the Bible to be historical fact that should be interpreted literally. Given this and given the subject of his *Appeal*, it is particularly interesting to note that he fails to consider the message in the book of Philemon. Philemon is the New Testament book that deals very directly with the subject of slavery. Walker is obviously very well-read, especially for a Negro in the early nineteenth century in America. His failure to consider Philemon can be assumed to be intentional. It is difficult to imagine that while he quotes numerous passages from Genesis to Revelation, he somehow misses Philemon. Why would he intentionally exclude its message? It is in this book that God explains his view on the relationship between freedom and the institution of slavery, and it is a message that calls into question Walker's justification for insurrection.

There are three characters in the book of Philemon—Paul the apostle, Philemon the Christian slave master, and Onesimus the runaway slave. Paul is writing a letter to Philemon, his friend and brother in the faith, about his runaway slave. Paul opens his letter with a prayer that Philemon will have a full understanding of every good thing there is to be had in Christ. Paul then appeals to him on behalf of Onesimus, and his love for the both of them. Onesimus had come to Rome after running away and there he encountered Paul. Through the relationship he developed with Paul, Onesimus had heard and accepted the message of the gospel and had become a Christian. Paul as he writes the letter is preparing to send Onesimus back to Philemon, back to slavery. He writes to remind Philemon what is required of him when dealing with his fellow Christian. "He [Onesimus] is very dear to me but even dearer to you, both as a man and as a brother in the Lord."[1]

The story is a very simple one. Philemon is one of the shortest books of the Bible with only 21 verses. So what can be the meaning Paul is trying to convey? If we take the text at face value, which Walker has urged us to do in every other instance, there are several things to note—the most important of which is the change in social relationships that occurs once Christ is accepted as savior and master. All other relationships become subordinate to the relationship one has with Christ. Paul in his letter to Philemon does not condemn or condone the institution of slavery. He rather argues for the "right" relationship between master and slave. If he can get Philemon to see the importance of relating to Onesimus as a brother in Christ (with love), treating him as he wishes to be treated, then the social relationship will take care of itself. As one relates to his/her fellow human with love then race, class, political affiliations, all those things that serve as psychological barriers between people cease to hold much significance. Paul emphasizes that through the power of love the walls that divide people can be broken down. Paul writes to the church at Colosse where Philemon is a member, "Here there is no Greek or Jew, circumcised or uncircumcised, barbarian, Scythian, slave or free, but Christ is all, and is in all."[2] All are equal in God's heart, and all relationships are made equal when one becomes a child of God. The standard by which one is to treat his/her brothers and sisters in Christ is to "love one another as Christ has loved you."

Walker cites a particular passage used as a tool by malicious pretenders to Christianity, "Slaves, obey your earthly masters with respect and fear, and with sincerity of heart."[3] However, there is a very significant part of the passage that has been left out by both Walker and those he criticizes. The full text reads:

> Slaves, obey your earthly masters with respect and fear, and with sincerity of heart, just as you would obey Christ. Obey them not only to win their favor when their eye is on you, but like slaves of Christ, doing the will of God from your heart. Serve wholeheartedly, as if you were serving the Lord, not men, because you know that the Lord will reward everyone for whatever good he does, whether he is slave or free. And masters, treat your slaves in the same way. Do not threaten them, since you know that he who is both their Master and yours is in heaven, and there is no favoritism with him.[4]

Reading it in its entirety we see that there are specific instructions given by Paul to both slaves and masters regarding their treatment of each other. Paul points to the accountability all will face regardless of their earthly positions without any hopes of favoritism. It is this principle of reward for obedience, obedience to the commands of God, which explains the treatment of Joseph discussed at length by Walker. Joseph was an Old Testament figure unjustly sold into slavery in Egypt by his jealous brothers, and yet because of his diligence in serving his masters and overseers, God elevated him to the social position of being second only to Pharaoh. The point both Paul and the story of Joseph emphasizes is that one is judged indiscriminately based upon one's obedience to God. Most specifically stressed is obedience to his command given in Leviticus and repeated by Jesus in the gospel of Matthew, "Love your neighbor as yourself."[5] The preachers Walker rightly criticizes fail to emphasize this principle of accountability because they are not challenging the legitimacy of the practice of slavery, nor do they wish to confront their own accountability. They are merely using the text to serve their personal interests without making any commitments to its core values. Walker unfortunately makes a similar mistake, although for very different reasons. Walker's interpretation, while committed to the core values represented, is colored by his desire to justify his praxis and convince those opposed to slavery to participate in insurrection.

However, it is not just the true nature of social relationships and the accountability all will face with respect to obedience to God that Paul addresses in the book of Philemon. There is also the important principle of reciprocity raised. In verse 19, Paul reminds Philemon that he owes his very self to Paul. Paul is known as the spiritual father of Philemon, as well as Onesimus who he refers to as son. This means that it was through Paul that Philemon was drawn into the faith and family of God. The reason this is significant is that it reminds Philemon that he himself had to be forgiven in order to become a child of God. The fact that he had to be forgiven encumbers him to be willing to forgive others, in this instance Onesimus. God expects reciprocity. What one receives from God, one is expected to extend to others—especially since none are deserving of God's grace and mercy.

Finally the book of Philemon teaches its readers something fundamental about the nature of true freedom. Onesimus must return as a runaway slave to his master and hope that he will be well-received. He must return in order to be freed from the bondage of slavery because being on the run does not constitute true freedom. Neither Paul nor Onesimus knew how Philemon would in fact receive his runaway slave; so the fact of enslavement was not of primary importance. The treatment of slave by master, and master by slave was the point emphasized. Does this mean that God is unconcerned with the institution of slavery? No, God gives too many commands regarding the treatment of others, none of which seem to indicate that bondage is a preferred practice. However, the proper understanding of how one is to rightly relate to his/her fellow human being is dependent upon first and foremost one's right relationship to God. True freedom requires that one trust God enough to accept, obey and allow him to sort out the social conditions and positions in which one finds oneself.

The requirement of obedience to God means that to accept Christ and the freedom he offers is not to enjoy absolute freedom. The freedom Christ offers has constraints—all of which have to do with maintaining a right relationship with him and others. This kind of freedom is born in hope and requires both courage and vulnerability because ultimately one's trust must be placed in God. There are no guarantees when it comes to how humans will behave. One must trust and hope that treating others as God requires will be rewarded, either in accordance with the principles of reciprocity or accountability. Consequently, this freedom is opposed to cynicism and fear. Cynicism and fear fueled by the value of self-interest both serve to color our worldviews and imprison our minds by making us unable to see the possibilities of what our world could be like.

Cynicism and fear dictate that we treat our fellow humans as if we must be suspicious of their motives because we cannot imagine that anyone would act out of something other than self-interest. We must read between the lines or below the surface to discover the true meaning of what is being said. Duplicity and hypocrisy have become the norm. Careful consideration born out of genuine concern for others is dismissed as idealistic and impractical. The value commitments we as Americans seem to have made to individualism has fostered within us a 'show me the money' or 'what's in it for me' mentality that relegates any level of concern for others to the area of philanthropy, which by definition is voluntary, not required or even expected.

The attractiveness of relativism has made our self-interest much more palatable than the alternative of absolute principles in that the values of others have no binding force on us. We have become so *free* as individuals that we are no longer free to commit ourselves uncompromisingly to any permanent and enduring universal principles. Furthermore, we have become as distrustful of our institutions as we are of each other. Consequently, we do not want government or other state organizations to take on the role of ensuring the general welfare because we are sure such practices will infringe upon our rights. This kind of freedom is more like a condemnation when we fail to recognize our lives must be understood in relationship to those with whom we live. We cannot live in a healthy and thriving society if the principles of equality, accountability and reciprocity are absent. We will continue as we are—vying for social position, shifting blame, and dodging responsibility—and we will continue to see our crises increase.

Freedom as liberty of the isolated individual must be rejected. We must reintroduce a concept of freedom that is firmly grounded in a stubborn optimism which challenges us to 'audaciously hope' and trust in the possibility of goodness in others and ourselves. A freedom that commits us to a pursuit of the common good as not just an abstract idea or overall state of affairs, but a common good that will be measured by how our neighbors are faring. When we are free to care about others and not just ourselves, we will have a model of true freedom to share with the world—a freedom that is worth fighting for.

Notes

1. Philemon 1:16.
2. Colossians 3:11.
3. Ephesians 6:5a.
4. Ephesians 6:5-9.
5. See Lev. 19:18 and Matt. 22:39.

Article IV
On Values

"I will walk about in freedom, for I have sought out your precepts."
Psalm 119:45

Values provide the framework for our worldview. They are the standards by which we measure and filter everything we encounter. Values shape our beliefs and attitudes, affect our feelings and responses, and influence our choices and actions. Therefore, what we value matters a great deal. Alain Locke, an African-American philosopher writing in the early twentieth century, makes the point that man cannot live in a world without values. He argues that all philosophies are ultimately philosophies of life and values, not philosophies of abstract or *objective* reality. This leads to his greater point that all philosophies have axiological implications—each presenting us with a system of values. Given the importance of the role that values play in the life of the human being, it would seem that one of the most important tasks for the philosopher to undertake is to engage in the study of value theory.

If there is anything we need to be contemplating critically, it is the basis, meaning, and consequences of the values that we hold. Philosophy as a discipline is perfectly situated to lead in this effort. However, we have allowed the philosophers of today to specialize in such narrowly focused sub-disciplines of philosophy that even they cannot see the connections between "their" area and other areas of philosophy. For example, the philosopher who specializes in metaphysics is often unable to see how it connects to epistemology, and neither the metaphysician nor the epistemologist sees the critical connections of those areas to value theory. Consequently it is becoming increasingly more difficult to convince ourselves and others of the relevance of philosophy for our everyday lives. We have quite successfully shown that the way we practice philosophy (ideological theorizing) has rendered it obsolete.

Plato in his well known work *The Republic* asserted that the philosopher has a duty that cannot be neglected.

> It is the duty of us, the founders, then, said I, to compel the best natures to at-
> tain the knowledge which we pronounced the greatest, and to win the vision of
> the good, to scale that ascent, and when they have reached the heights and
> taken an adequate view, we must not allow what is now permitted . . . That they
> [the philosophers who arise among us] should linger there, I said, and refuse to

go down again among those bondsmen and share their labors and honors,
whether they are of less or of greater worth.[1]

Plato denies the philosopher the option of remaining outside the cave and bask-
ing in the light of his/her own enlightenment, engaging only in conversations
with other philosophers. Instead the philosopher must return to the cave to at-
tempt to free the slaves and unmask the 'idols'.

Rather than taking up this duty, too many of the philosophers today would
rather stay in the proverbial ivory tower, writing and producing philosophy for
other philosophers. Perhaps many feel that the more inaccessible their work is to
the society at large, the better their work must be. This has resulted in the public
discourse being guided not by the best minds we have to offer but by the politicians who are wrangling for office, the political pundits, the biased media, and
the predatory preachers. Furthermore, we have failed to provide the public with
the skills for critically evaluating the diverse and divergent information with
which they are presented.

We see so much semantic shuffling and fast stepping that it is unclear what
our terms even mean now. We in fact have no fixed content of our values any-
more. Terms such as right and wrong, good and bad, free and oppressed, torture
and interrogate signify nothing in particular. We parse and redefine terms so
often that we have divested, not merely obfuscated, them of meaning. Today
democracy looks more like empire-building or at least bullying, and justice
looks more like special interest. And who even knows what *truth* is? In a world
where meaning is unclear, we are unable to find a moral or even consistent
framework by which we guide our lives. Moreover, we have no firm convictions
that make it possible to construct such a framework. Human life is most fundamentally marked by choice, and we need something firm, an anchor if you will,
to guide us in making those choices. In such a world where the job of philosophers may be to reestablish the possibility that words can have meaning and that
truth can be enduring, we as philosophers do not have the luxury of just philoso-
phizing. We cannot settle for just being gadflies. It seems that our job has to be
much more demanding.

When we consider the conditions we find in the *first world*, in a wealthy
nation such as ours where over 47 million people lack adequate health care and
that number is increasing, where tragically large numbers of people are dying of
conditions such as asthma, a controllable and treatable disease, we should be
terrified. When considering conditions like these, some important questions
need to be asked. Philosophers have important work to do. We need to ask questions that have the chance of changing our worldviews. *What do we value?*
How do our values shape the community — the world in which we live?

A few years ago I participated in a panel discussion on the moral imperatives for better health care and education. This particular panel took place on the
second day of a conference, the tenth annual Philosophy Born of Struggle conference that focused on rethinking the intellectual life. The first day's thought
provoking presentations had me seriously contemplating the intellectual life of

the philosopher. I was left pondering what important things there are to say about moral imperatives for better health care and education and what this might have to do with the intellectual life. This issue is quite relevant today as we engage in discourse about universal health care. I first considered whether there were such things as moral imperatives and decided yes, I believe there are. But really, so what? I was among philosophers who came from a variety of ethical positions and knew that it was unlikely to say the least that we would come to an agreement in one afternoon or one lifetime on the precise articulation of such an imperative, even if we all began by agreeing there was one to be articulated. The fact is that we live in a world that as it is becoming more and more globalized, thereby drawing people closer together, is at the same time becoming more and more divided in terms of our ideologies.

Alain Locke said almost 100 years ago, before the super highway known as the internet and before satellite television, that as our proximity to others around the world increases, our psychological distance also increases. Unfortunately, we do not share a connectedness, even within our own society that allows us to agree on very much at all, especially with regard to ethical issues. So, what would be the real benefit of articulating a particular moral imperative for anything, if what we seek to achieve is to offer something important that may aid in the effort to heal humanity, or at the very least help bring about the tangible results of better health care?

After thinking about this for a period of time I have concluded that in truth the moral imperative is not what needs to be articulated at this time. To suppose that the imperative will help us in our struggle to achieve better health care, or anything else for that matter, is to presuppose something that is not necessarily true—namely that people in general really do care about other people. As I look around the world, as I look around our own society, I do not see the evidence of our sincere care for others. The moral imperative that may be articulated, regardless of the form it takes—whether it is developed within the framework of an ethics of personal accountability or presents itself as an *a priori* rational principle in a duty-based ethics, or even a command given by divine authority—will be powerless to save the society, the world, and humanity.

The imperative cannot save the ordinary people, the people in our own society who are without adequate health care. In the case of health care, we have seen the response of a number of employers to policies which mandate they provide certain levels of health care for their employees. In the cases where it has been deemed to negatively affect the profit margin, the employers simply lay off those workers who are then uninsured and unemployed, pack up and move to some other location, oftentimes overseas. We call this outsourcing—and it has a tragic effect in a society where quality of life is directly tied to one's ability to work. Furthermore, in an economy such as our current one, unemployment is a condemnation to poverty. We see currently the problem ordinary people have procuring affordable prescription drugs. Too often people are forced to choose between filling their prescriptions and paying their utility bills because the profit margins of the American pharmaceutical companies are more important than the health of the citizens they seek to serve. In both of these cases we see the conflict between profit and life.

The moral imperative cannot save the policy-makers because they cannot live up to it. There can be no real and sustained commitment made when such commitments are ultimately contingent upon financial and political support offered. On the one hand, the politician who sees the office sought as the greater good is not interested in making sincerely firm commitments because they do not serve him/her well. On the other hand, the politician who asserts the importance of sincere commitments regardless of what that means in terms of campaign funding is labeled naïve and lacking in political savvy. The real issue is again about values. Our problems are not problems of politics but problems of values. The important questions with regard to employment, education and health insurance is *do we really care about others?* The philosopher needs to bring this question to the forefront. Perhaps being confronted with the very basic question do *you* really care about others and being pushed to answer it can wake people up and cause them to reorient themselves, to refocus on what it would mean to care.

As stated earlier, it is no longer enough for philosophers to aspire to be gadflies. It seems that we would do better to act as defibrillators to revive the public consciousness that has become flat-lined, as philosopher Thomas Slaughter so aptly put it. The philosopher must encourage and lead us in the study of our values if we hope to transform our society. Drawing people's awareness to the issues will not be enough. We need to learn how to evaluate and analyze our issues. The problems of health care, education and the economy are not problems of policy confined to the political arena. They are most fundamentally problems of values.

Being confronted with suffering has not made a significant difference in present or past times. We need to provide better health care not because we have finally become convinced on rational grounds of some moral imperative to do so. We need to do it because we care about and value the lives of our fellow human beings. We cannot be centered on personal gratification, thereby allowing ourselves to be controlled by the market. We cannot believe that our only power comes from self-determination. We have for too long been driven by values such as personal gratification and self-determination that are in direct contradiction to the values and principles of equality and fairness that we espouse. In the worst case, this makes us hypocrites. In the mildest case, it makes us slaves who believe that the satisfaction of our desires sooner rather than later, and the freedom to live without constraints are worthwhile ideals to be pursued at all costs.

This inconsistency in principles espoused and actual values pursued, both past and present, is what made the practice of slavery possible for those great minds who articulated so eloquently the fundamental principles of human liberty. It is this inconsistency that is also responsible for the current social crises in which we find ourselves. Our current debates regarding freedom and how it should be defined often touch upon the sore point of proper principles or values.

Questions such as *does freedom require a specific political context* and *does freedom require a free market society* are important to ponder. Those who would answer these questions in the affirmative seem to suggest that freedom at its essence is experienced most fully at the level of the individual. Oppression in any form is defined and identified as problematic because it restricts the fundamental freedom to make what we will of ourselves. However, the answer to those questions may not be yes.

We see today the same kind of commitment to determining our own fate and our right to economic independence as was present in the eighteenth and nineteenth centuries. We seem to be wholly committed to a faith in our own individual free will. We do not really question so much this principle of freedom of the will to determine our own fate. We tend to focus more on the consequences of imagined possibilities rather than on the actual principles driving them. Take for example the situation in Iraq; we will argue about the consequences of the actions of our free will, i.e. how much money we are spending in Iraq and how many U.S. soldiers have died. We fail too often, however, to inquire about the *fundamental* reasons we got into the war and why we allowed it to escalate to the degree that it has. And those who do raise the question are likely to have their patriotism questioned.

It is our failure to investigate our own positions and practices critically that leads to inconsistency in many instances. Recent findings indicate that this is something with which we still struggle on a large scale in our society. One interesting example can be found in the context of religion where the inconsistencies are especially pronounced. The Pew Forum in August 2008 released its findings regarding a survey of the United States religious landscape.[2] It found that with respect to our approach to faith, we are quite non-dogmatic. We tend to shape our theology to fit our culture, rather than using theology as a basis for shaping our culture. Open-mindedness is deemed to be more valuable than committing to religious absolutes. Religious devotion is seen by the majority as being in conflict with living in a modern society. The desire to absolutely avoid dogmatism is at odds with securing the objective moral framework many deem as necessary to provide stability to our society. While religion is seen as being critically important and relevant to our individual lives, it is not viewed as being important enough to provide the society at large with meaningful guidance. It is much more important that everyone be free to choose for themselves, without constraints, what they pledge their loyalty to and what they value.

Such ideas of freedom, because of their emphasis on the individual, fail to provide us with the necessary guiding principles to be of much use in today's context. They tend to lead us to pursuing narrowly conceived methods for securing freedom. The method tends to be goal-oriented in nature. For the abolitionist the goal was emancipation which did not bring about the desired freedom. For small colonies it was national independence. And for current defenders of freedom, it was at first the removal of Saddam, then it was Iraqi elections, now it is stability and the ability of Iraqis to defend themselves, and so on. The bar is not fixed but is in a constant state of flux because our principles and value commitments are ever-changing. Also problematic is that the attainment of the goals that are set is said to require political savvy. Those people without the forces of money and influence must today be skilled politicians because problems are viewed in essence as political in nature. The problem with this is that history shows us politics tends to obscure truth and justice, not ensure them.

Locke in the same piece quoted at the beginning of this chapter identified the greatest challenge for the twentieth century philosopher as finding a way to establish an objective guide for values without falling into dogmatism and intolerance. We have succeeded in part. We have found a way to avoid dogmatism and intolerance in many cases, but we have failed to find an objective guide for our values. In our effort to avoid dogmatism we have failed to make any meaningful value commitments that foster the health and well-being of society. We have done so by denying the possibility that specific values may have objective status and bring about universal benefit. It is the pursuit of this question regarding the possibilities of values that the philosopher must engage in through the study of value theory. Only by finding such values will we be able to articulate a concept of freedom that really does apply universally.

Notes

1. Edith Hamilton and Huntington Cairns (eds.), Plato: The Collected Dialogues, (Princeton: Princeton University Press, 1989), p. 751-752, Plato's Republic 519 c-d.
2. The Pew Forum on Religion & Public Life, The Demographics of Faith, Report, August 2008.

Index

Author Bio

Daphne M. Rolle received her Ph.D. from Purdue University, where she studied under Dr. Leonard Harris, in 2002. She now teaches African-American Philosophy and American Philosophy at Ball State University. She lives in central Indiana with her husband and two children.

www.ingramcontent.com/pod-product-compliance
Lightning Source LLC
Chambersburg PA
CBHW030657270326
41929CB00007B/411